As much as we pretend otherwise, we want what's comfortable, and we're afraid of the different. We're afraid of change.

—FRANK GEHRY

This book is available for bulk purchasing as well as for educational uses. For more information please send an email to info@mrdabney.com

Finding One

FINDING ONE'S SELF AMIDST SOCIETAL NORMS,
DIGITAL LIFE, AND PURSUING GOALS

VAUGHN DABNEY

CONTENTS

DEDICATION

For my mother who always allowed me to be my own person and for showing me what perseverance looks like. The entrepreneur I am today is owed to her. And my sister for being my Sunshine.

In loving memory of Keith and Christina.

ACKNOWLEDGMENTS

Thank you to my mother again, for giving me the ability needed to get to where I am today...I love you more than you know. Thank you to both of my grandmothers for making sure I ate well as a growing young man building my many lego houses and drawing cartoon characters. Thank you to everyone who told me over the years that I needed to write a book. This is because of you that I now have something tangible. Thank you to Brian Wilson for teaching me how to harness the power of communication. You've taught me so many things since we first met as teenagers. I am he. And he is me. You have always impressed me with your capacity to speak to people. Thank you to Daé for encouraging me and supporting me through this process. Thanks to Alex Elle for always being a catalyst in some of my creative endeavors. Thanks to Lucy Dazilma for writing her book before I got to mine and inspiring me to get on it! Finally, thank you to the universe for teaching me. I feel you Karma.

INTRODUCTION

I'm just going to jump right in. This book is about finding yourself.

It's a culmination of various social posts, thoughts, opinions, experiences, and observations from my life. Things that have carried me through so many challenges and moments of adversity. After being told many times that I should write a book...I have.

I've lived in many places: Oregon, Texas, Georgia, Ohio, and California. Some of these places were by choice, others were necessary. I went to five different elementary schools growing up so I never had those life long friends that a lot of people do when they've grown up in the same place their entire life. When I was young I think this affected me a little. To no one's fault, I would just go with it and we would move again. By the second or third time though...something inside of me created an excitement. I would actually look forward to moving and meeting/making new friends. Regardless of how long I may know them, it forced me to maximize my connections. It also made me extremely sensitive to people's energy at a young age. Being able to discern between good and bad intentions was so valuable.

Taking all of this and translating it to my now 32 year old

self (at the time of writing this), I wouldn't have my childhood experiences, or any experiences for that matter, changed one bit. It shaped me. Although I have more stability than my 7 year old self, I still enjoy moving, traveling, and being immersed in foreign places. It's an advantage that allows me to capitalize on the bleakest of outlooks and situations.

Everything in this book is what I believe and practice. Everything. My energy and soul as a logic-driven person will seep through the words you are about to read. Know that they come from a place of care and love.

THE EGO & SELF

GET OUT OF YOUR FUCKING FEELINGS, FOCUS ON YOUR GOALS, AND MAKE SHIT HAPPEN.

Often times we're subjected to the constraints, expectations, and standards of others, when really -- they don't matter. The opinions of your family, your significant other, and friends are just that...opinions. If you're successful, get used to people saying things you don't want to hear. Commentators will always be present. Be worried if they're not saying anything!

Actions & Reflections

What are some goals you'd like to achieve this week?

In six months?

One year?

Keep going. Set your vision.

STOP TAKING THINGS PERSONALLY

It took me a while to understand this concept and it's something that must be learned alone in your time of peace. Acknowledge how you feel when you are in harmony. Take this feeling and use it as a reference of how you want to feel all the time.

No one can MAKE you feel any kind of way with their actions. It is within ourselves that we manifest feelings based off of our expectations and values of self, thus projecting and expecting the same from those around us.

When those standards are encroached upon, our learned responses kick in and the reaction is to get offended. "How could someone so close hurt my feelings?" You have to change that way of thinking for this to work. I won't say every time, but the majority of other people's verbal/emotional/psychological attacks on you come from a deficit within themselves. It could be because of self-esteem, insecurity, envy, the need for attention, or a lack of love (self love as well as from those around them).

Knowing this, you are empowered. Take a step back when someone is attacking your peace and breathe. Breathe again. Then assess what may be happening within that person and perhaps reach out to them to help. Maybe all they need is an embrace from someone.

Remember...

It's not always about you.

Actions & Reflections

Do you easily get offended or take things personally?

How do you usually handle the situation?

Being at peace and not taking things personally doesn't mean you don't or won't feel anything when these situations occur. It's all about how you handle the situation that will allow you to transcend meaningless turbulence to create meaningful connections on a higher level. Keep communication open.

You are strong. You are resilient. You yield only to what you allow your mind to accept.

HUMILITY

Be humble. Not to be confused with a lack of confidence in your gifts and presence. Stand tall so crowns don't fall. But keep humility in your back pocket. You can always learn something and despite what you may think, you got to where you're at because of the help of others. Before you yell out that you made it on your own, really think about that. And when you get to the top of your mountain, reach back down with open arms. We must let go of the 'only me' mentality.

Actions & Reflections

Think about where you're at in your life. Who helped you along the way?

Do you think you'd be in the same position/level of achievement if those people had not been there?

When is the last time you showed gratitude to those people or anyone in your life just because? Do that now. At this moment. Whomever you thought of while reading this is who should hear from you. No text messages either.

Everyone is in your life for a specific reason and if you neglect to acknowledge those who've allowed you to step on their shoulders, the universe will expect much more from you later on.

COMPARISON

I've noticed something that is progressively getting worse. People are competing with each other over hair, relationships, cars, business acumen, life...this is why so few are making the majority of the money. It's bullshit and it hurts my heart. Wake up. Be better than YOU were yesterday instead of trying to outshine others today. You'll get much further working together. Until you drop that "only me" mentality, you're never going to win. Ever.

OWN YOUR SHIT. THE GOOD AND THE BAD.

ACCOUNTABILITY

Taking responsibility for your actions is one of the most important things you can do for yourself as well as the people around you. No one likes a "blamer". You know...that person who blames his/her problems on external factors or everyone else but themselves. Only you control what decisions you make. When you make a choice, own that choice. Accept what outcomes may happen and move forward. You need to be responsible for that shit. Disappointment comes from having expectations of others and not of yourself.

Change your mentality right now.

LISTENING TO YOURSELF

Listen to yourself. Listen to what your energy tells you. Listen to what people show you. The truth is always there, you just have to be willing to accept it. Consciousness is imperative. Listen to your heart. Listen when it tells you to stop. Listen when it tells you to go. Listen when it gives you feelings of uncertainty or confidence. Intuition is something we've all been blessed with. It's up to us to use it.

STOP COMPLAINING. NO ONE CARES.

No one cares if you don't like your job. No one cares if your day isn't going well. No one cares if things aren't going well. No one cares about these things, IF you're not trying to change/improve/better the situations you are facing. Consolation can only go so far, but the next question from your friends listening to you complain should be, "So what are you doing about xyz?"

GOALS & ACHIEVEMENT

NO REGRETS

Embracing any kind of regret is disrespectful to your life journey. Stop it. Things happen as they should and the universe has put you in a place to reflect and learn, not to regret. If you changed one thing from that one incident, how do you know your life would be better? Perhaps it may have presented new issues unforeseen. You just don't know and you'll never know. This fact alone should illustrate the wasted energy that goes into having regrets. Acknowledge, learn, and keep moving.

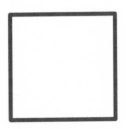

Actions & Reflections

Step 1

Write all your regrets in the outlined box. If they overlap each other it's ok.

Step 2

Now, focus on the boundary in which the box confines your regrets.

Step 3

Now visualize yourself inside the box.

Step 4

This is what having regrets does to your mind -- limitations and lack of clarity.

Step 5

Take a black marker or pen and color in the box so you can no longer see the words of past. Don't allow your light to shine on anything that inhibits your growth and greatness.

BE FEARLESS

You must be fervent. You must be relentless. You must embrace failure and be fearless in your pursuit of whatever you want in this life. Better to have tried and failed than to have not tried at all.

Actions & Reflections

What are you afraid of?

_____

_____

Why are you afraid? What's stopping you from metaphorically jumping into what you want to do?

_____

_____

However rational or irrational these fears may seem, they are valid. Acknowledge them. Now devise a plan to overcome them one step at a time. Consistency and time paired with the belief in yourself is how you do this. Be patient with you.

PROCRASTINATION

Do what is asked of you (or what you ask of yourself) as soon as possible if not immediately. Why wait? Procrastination is inconsiderate. Procrastination is wasteful. Procrastination is a dream killer. The aforementioned applies to yourself as well as others. Really ask yourself next time, "Is there a need for me to wait?", if you can't honestly answer with a yes, then do it now. What are you waiting for?

FAILURE

Raise your hand if you enjoy failing? I'll wait.... No one likes to fail but in my opinion it's a necessary step in order to achieve your goals.   Notice I didn't attribute the necessity to fail with success? This is because success is relative to the individual. Often times we mistakenly compare ourselves to others in our industry — big mistake. Your struggles, your environment, and your resources are your own. This is what makes personal success a beautiful thing. You only need to meet the standards set by you.   When you fail, this is the time to hold yourself accountable, but more importantly acknowledge why you failed.

The ticket to reaching your goals is to be comfortable with failure. When we can see our goals, what's the first thing we possibly ask ourselves? "How do I get there?" or "Who do I need to introduce myself to?" These are questions that lead you towards success.

Actions & Reflections

Below, I have listed common questions to target your goals and determine if you need to raise the bar for yourself:

When is the last time you were rejected or ignored in an attempt to reach a goal?

When you are rejected or ignored, do you try again?

Failing is always a step closer than not trying at all.

Have your recent achievements or endeavors been easy to obtain?

Basking in the waters of inaction is the most detrimental thing you can do and a quick way to fall short. You want to be able to say that you tried and failed.

COMFORT ZONES

More often than not, we get comfortable. We're content with life but we call ourselves ambitious. If you're reading this, you want to grow and you are ready to change your current state. I implore you to step outside of that comfort zone. For me it has been making cold calls, emailing fortune 500 CEOs, or starting a dialogue with business owners on social media. Possibilities are endless and I'm sure you can think of something that you've never done before that may help you.

Here's an actual example of when I stepped outside of my comfort zone:

I was a college graduate getting ready to move 600 miles away to Atlanta, Georgia to start my journey of being a freelance web developer. I had a friend there (forever grateful) who let me stay with her until I was able to afford living on my own. I knew that ultimately, my goal was to start his my business. Once I arrived, this is what I thought about:

How can I make money here?

What can I do to possibly start my business now?

What is the market like for the type of business I want to do?

I needed a way to hit the ground running. This is how I did it:

I started by checking Craigslist every day since he was familiar with it from high school (I remember when there was only about seven cities listed!). I figured it was a great temperature gauge for markets in most major cities. If I saw anything that was relevant to web development, I'd respond. This was the routine every day.

I polished up my resume and posted it on all the major job sites such as: Monster, Indeed, and Career Builder—this was before LinkedIn became the go to.

I made a list of marketing companies, ad agencies, and local businesses categorized by the aesthetic of their websites, then proceeded to call them. This is what's called cold calling – when you call a business unsolicited. I'd say, "Hey, my name is Vaughn Dabney, I'm a local web professional and I was wondering if you were looking to redesign your website." Responses consisted of: "No we're not interested.", "What do you mean, we just had it redesigned?" Click, dial tones and so on.

Eventually, I got a hit on the résumé sites from a staffing agency which led to a full-time job with MySpace just after three months. This was the most uncomfortable thing I've ever had to do. Calling these companies and trying to persuade them to let me redesign their site sounded so insane, but I was motivated (and desperate as a college graduate). I wanted to be in the industry in which I was interested – software and web development. This required me to step out of my comfort zone. I had a job, but I wanted something more for myself. My story isn't any better or different from any other person trying to reach their goals. They will all tell you that at some point, they were forced to step outside their comfort zone to get to the top.

STAYING MOTIVATED

Once you get to where you're going, how do you stay there? How do you build momentum to maintain your current pace to jump again? Know this: there is always someone watching every move you make. Someone you are motivating or inspiring. When you're successful, they experience success too. Being conscious of this, you start to feel yourself perform on new levels. It feels good to inspire people. Positivity is infectious. When you motivate others, you inadvertently motivate yourself because after all, you are on a journey- to reach the level of success that you've set for yourself. A level beyond your comfort zones in which you inevitably fail until you get it right or figure out another approach. If you've given everything you have and just can't seem to get there, it may not be for you. And that's okay. Your character is strengthened when you can accept what is not for you. But as long as you continue forward, seeking new goals to achieve, you will always remain on the path toward success.

MANIFESTATION

The moment you put a thought into the universe it will begin to manifest. You have planted the seed. How much you water it is up to you. This goes for both positive and negative energy. Are you nurturing the right thoughts? Or is your metaphysical garden full of disease?

GET UNCOMFORTABLE

One of the most important lessons I've learned as an entrepreneur is to be uncomfortable. To put myself in positions in which I am yielded different results. When pattern like behavior starts to show, switch it up. For me it was cold calling or going out and actively marketing my company. On a daily basis though, I make it a point to go out to a bar or restaurant by myself and talk to people. I'm in the house all day working and my social skills need to stay sharp -- this helps. At first it can be a little unnerving and you may feel like people are judging you for having a beer by yourself. They are. But that will always be the case. Who cares? Embrace the "me" time and just be. Meet some strangers!

ARE YOU A ONE CUP PERSON OR DO YOU HAVE A FEW?

Don't worry. Keep reading, it'll all make sense.

Someone once asked me, "Vaughn, how do you focus on so many goals at the same time and yet you still seem to complete each one?" Something to that effect. I really had to think about this. After all, this is something that comes naturally to me and a few others I know.

Let's take a look at what most people do and are told to do. Most of us are told early on to "focus on one thing" and when you finish that, you can start something else. This works for most. Less stress, full focus, and usually solid results. These are people who focus on *one cup*.

At the other end of the spectrum, you have people who can handle multiple projects at once...people who have *multiple cups*. They usually, like myself, have been doing this for most of their lives. However, I had a very hard time explaining how I was able to manage AND complete my projects other than using words like "diligence" or "consistency". This trait is not to be confused with individuals who start many projects or endeavors and never finish them.

You are probably asking yourself, "What does this have to do with cups though? I've also been asked how I respond to people who think focusing on multiple things is associated with lack of focus. My response? It's like filling up cups of water.

For the single project people: you are filling one cup of water at a time. When you've finished, you grab another cup and repeat the process.

For the multi-project people: you have many cups and you're filling each one a little at a time. Similar to how a bartender lines up shot glasses end-to-end and pours the tequila in a sweeping motion between the first and last glasses. Eventually they all fill to the top, it just takes longer than an individual glass. This is the concept.

This analogy has stuck with me ever since. It makes sense to me and others who are like this. However, it wasn't until I read an article on Forbes by Ryan Blair* and it hit me; one word that brought on the "eureka moment" — *compartmentalization*. The idea that one can compartmentalize or isolate specific tasks/projects in separate mental containers. So as not to interfere with a task at hand, but making it readily available for access at a moment's notice. The article's author is far more eloquent than I am so I encourage you to read it. It spoke volumes to me and it's something that I realized but I didn't know how to express it.

So far it's worked for me and according to the article, it's key to being a successful entrepreneur. Whichever method you are comfortable with, take that and run with it. Successful people come from different walks of life and only you know what works for you.

"IF YOU WANT TO GO FAST, GO ALONE.

IF YOU WANT TO GO FAR, GO TOGETHER"

This is an African proverb that resonates with me and speaks volumes to how some people operate. If you want to go faster than anyone else, do it alone. If you want to go further, go together. Get a team behind you. Get some support. Understand that you cannot achieve the greatest goals by yourself.

RELATIONSHIPS

FOCUS ON WHAT MATTERS

Don't get so hyper-focused on issues that you end up finding something wrong with everything. In fact, you can "spin" anything to be your truth.

Perception is reality.

If you look for something, you may just find it. This is like a "hyper-manifestation" that you're creating—like a self-fulfilling prophecy. Usually it happens when you don't want something to happen, so you obsess about it (watering your garden) and give it the energy needed to cultivate. Soon, you see the fruition take place followed by, "I knew this would happen.".

You made that shit happen. Our energy has the power to do this.

Tighten up and be aware of what you're putting out into the universe.

ACTIVE LISTENING FOR RELATIONSHIPS

Learn how to listen. More often than not, we are so consumed by what we're going to say next during conversations. Really, we should be focused on what the other person is saying. Listen and then let them know you were listening by asking relevant questions or summarizing what they just said.

Everyone wants to be heard.

BE CLEAR WITH YOUR INTENTIONS.

BANKING

The type of banking I'm referring to is ***emotional banking***. When is the last time you made a deposit into someone's emotional bank account? What does this mean? Simply put—intangible accounts and connections that are created when you form relationships with people (personal or professional).

Naturally, that takes us into the idea of withdrawals and deposits. **An emotional withdrawal can be one of three things:**

> 1. Doing something to hinder the transcendence or growth of a relationship (e.g. always *taking* instead of giving*)*

> 2. Constantly asking the other person for something (time, support, etc) without reciprocity (see #1)

3. When your presence is rare and inconsistent

An emotional deposit is when you add something to a relationship:

1. Giving to the other person (time, support, etc)

2. Showing love, kind gestures out of nowhere

3. Consistency in presence

With emotional deposits, your relationships grow and flourish, unlike withdrawals that do the exact opposite. So ultimately, the more you invest, the more you can ask of the other person since you have more "emotional money" in the bank. But be careful not to withdrawal so much that you end up with a negative balance. Overdraft fees are real. Emotional ones are worse than the monetary fees we're used to. It's that one little request or withdrawal that takes you just below a zero balance and causing chaos. You not only have a negative emotional balance, but you have a fee added on top. That fee could be in the form of that person not feeling like you're there for them. All because you took more than you gave.

Now you have to work harder to get back into the good

graces of that particular person.

Today, invest in the people you love. Tell friends and family you love and care for them. Do things that are unexpected. Those gestures have the most weight to the people you care about.

Four play is necessary.

NOSTALGIA

Nostalgia is beautiful. Don't block your memories. Be they positive or negative, good or bad, they are part of the formula that created your identity.

EMOTIONAL FLEXIBILITY

I've learned that sometimes my logical mind needs to take a break and cater to other's emotions. During times of personal crisis, practicality is necessary but so is *hope*. Giving someone hope can mean the difference between a beautiful recovery and complete psychological destruction. Humans need hope. We need something to reach for when dealing with adversity. It's a mindset powerful enough to uplift an entire culture.

Give people hope.

FORGIVENESS

You will forever be miserable until you learn to forgive people that matter to you.

Forgive someone today.

Actions & Reflections

Who can you forgive today, without conditions, and without apologies from either person?

What kind of feelings have you harbored because you haven't forgiven people in your life?

What about yourself? We often live with guilt because we haven't accepted our own mistakes.

COME BACK

Turn off your notifications. Connect with the world again. Go outside and play. You don't need to see notifications from every social media network. You may feel naked and even afraid that you'll miss something but you won't. You'll be at peace. I can't tell you how many people I'm around that literally cannot hold conversations because they need to be on the phone. This is just silly. Get off your phone and learn what it means to be with people.

COMMUNICATION

THE LINE OF COMMUNICATION

When forming new relationships with people, whether romantic, personal, or professional, we must make it a point to establish the foundation for an open and clear line of communication. As with anything we must set the bar in the beginning in order to operate smoothly throughout the course of said relationship. This can usually be accomplished by making ourselves transparent and vulnerable (when you feel you're ready). Express and address topics and issues that you are comfortable with. In turn, the receiving person will likely mimic what they hear, similar to body language. When done correctly, there's less chance of any miscommunication or assumptions to occur.

Actions & Reflections

Can you think of a specific event or relationship in which you fe't the communication wasn't where it needed to be?

If yes, did you ever identify the root issue for the miscommunication?

Although we have different levels of relationships, the importance and routine of setting up clear lines of communication should be paramount and unchanging. By creating a habit, you don't have to think about it…it just happens.

SAYING NO

Whether it's with business or personal relationships, it's important to learn how to say "no" and be okay with that. Everyone knows how difficult it can be, especially with the factors that play into decision making. Being able to say this word is essential to you as well as the people asking for something.

Life decisions can be broken down into a binary system: "I'm going to do it" (yes) or "I'm not going to do it" (no). Two choices, one decision. Most people say "yes" much too often when they should really be saying "no". It's usually to the people closest to us that we have a problem turning down requests. Or perhaps we want acceptance within a group of acquaintances (peer pressure). We don't want them to feel like they can't ask for anything or maybe we want to be in good standing, all the time. It happens in business relationships too. The reality is, you can't please everyone. Periodically, someone has to get the short-end of the stick. Once you master the art of saying "no", you will see a few things happen:

People will start to respect your time,

People will start to respect your decisions, and

You will develop a clarity for decision making because guilt or personal favor won't be the influencers of said decisions.

The best approach to change how often you oblige people, is to ease into it. Don't start saying "no" to everything because you want to make a stance. This is a change of moderation. Continue to say "yes" to small things you don't mind doing. The moment you feel like you really shouldn't or can't help someone, listen to that feeling and speak the words, "no". Of course there are variations such as: "Oh, I'm sorry I just really can't help you with this", "If I could I would, but [insert actual reasons]", or "I would probably be doing you a disservice if I helped. I just don't feel like it". That last one is for the bold readers. Ultimately, you want the people around you to gradually experience the change.

Watch out for people who have mastered the "guilt-trip" (this includes children). Not to be confused with feeling guilty from a simple request. When a person induces feelings of chagrin or shame because you have no capacity to help them, that's what's considered a guilt trip. When you notice this, ask questions to see what the person's motives are. Your better judgment will override a "no" response if the person actually needs you. The signs will be there.

Above all, remain conscious and objective of how you feel when making decisions. It will lead to a settling in your energy and you will feel good about the decisions you've made since they were made with the best intentions. Again, you cannot please everyone all the time. Be selective and don't be afraid to say "no".

WE MUST LEARN HOW TO COMMUNICATE EFFECTIVELY AND HONESTLY. IT'S THE HIGHEST FORM OF CURRENCY IN OUR RELATIONSHIPS.

When you can clearly communicate your wants and needs, life is much easier. You remove the air of assumption and make room for clarity. All of your relationships should have clear, honest, and open communication.

r

ANTAGONISTIC RESPONSES

Sometimes when in arguments or heated discussions, we may speak in a manner that is antagonistic instead of productive. The goal of every argument or discussion should be to understand usually by presenting our case, whether it's how we feel about the topic or by using facts. We ultimately desire the other persons understanding and/or compassion despite the fact they may disagree with our viewpoint.

Instead of saying a smart comment, stay on track. Focus on what is happening at the moment and what is being discussed instead of saying something tangential or off topic. This can give rise to a couple circumstances: the receiving person is upset you've added complexity to the argument or they could be hurt/angry by what you said.

Keep it clean and concise.

PASSIVE AGGRESSIVENESS

Saying things just to get a response instead of the results you actually want is PASSIVE AGGRESSIVENESS in its ugliest form. This is not the way to communicate when you have an issue that needs resolution. This includes posting on social media…in fact let's address this deeper. This is one of the most detrimental forms of P.A. because you're now involving anyone who can see your post. The last thing you want is for people to wonder about personal problems that you have not yet resolved. When I was younger I probably did this and I think everyone has at one point. It's almost like therapy though, because you want to be "heard" by the person whom it's directed towards, but also from your peers who may possibly provide a sympathetic "digital shoulder". However, it usually backfires and your message never gets delivered properly. Another form of P.A. includes asking questions you already know the answer to (rhetorical). This behavior could fit neatly in the previous section of being *antagonistic*.

COMMUNICATION

The best way to handle personal issues is offline, but more importantly, to be direct with your communication. Express your feelings directly with the person.

Don't trade clear communication for ambiguous comments that could: 'potentially be towards someone but not quite because you didn't mention their name'.

It may take some time but being direct and honest is the best way to be.

AVOID WAITING TO RESOLVE PROBLEMS

Hopefully when you have a problem, your next course of action is to solve it, regardless of size and scale. Otherwise, when these issues, even small ones, build up, they're bound to spill out eventually…usually at the wrong time.

What happens is that these little problems don't really bother us because we feel the need to be accepting of each other's flaws and work with them right? Yes and no. Accepting enough to where we don't have a society full of superficial people (too late?) and not accepting to where the other person is being disrespectful or discourteous to you.

[Enter handful of said problems] — now you have this heavy load on your conscious. It shows in your actions, it's heard in your tone of voice, and it affects you in countless other ways. But that's not the worst part. When the last scale-tipping problem is introduced, you unleash everything that's been trapped inside. This usually causes a disproportionate response to whatever is happening. The receiving person experiences the following:

1. Confusion - they don't know what the hell is happening. They thought the argument was going to be about the dirty dishes in the sink.

2. Unfair advantage - one cannot defend themselves from their past actions from weeks or months ago that were never brought up at the time of said actions.

Because this person you're unloading on has lost their bearings and cannot recount what *you* remember so vividly, things are blown out of proportion.

It's usually a terrible situation that can go a lot smoother with proper communication of feelings.

Actions & Reflections

For people that have a tendency to let things build up and fester instead of letting them out:

- Practice addressing problems as they happen. I'm not saying on the first time something happens per se, but if you notice a pattern, speak up. Otherwise, you have to let it go. It's just not fair.

- When you feel like there are a few things that have built up, have a sit-down talk with the other person. That way, you're not waiting for something else to happen (however convenient it may be) before you decide to drop a bomb.

For the people that are or have been on the receiving end of this:

- Try to really listen to what the other person is saying, taking note of what bothers them, including their body language during the build-up phase. You can try and diffuse the situation by asking, "hey is something wrong?"

- If it's just too late and you are in the midst of it, try keeping your cool and pointing out that you can't defend what happened in the past since you didn't realize it was an issue. But that moving forward, you will be more conscious of it.

It takes patience and understanding from both sides.

When you feel like you're going to

complain or need to complain,

remember:

change is what you seek, not sympathy

ENERGY

YOUR BEING IS SACRED

Being extremely discerning about who you allow into your space. Be it your personal space, your home (especially your home), your car, your "circle"...

You must build harmony within yourself and around you so that you can identify disruption. Exercise and practice removing toxic individuals and experiences. Full force. It can be especially difficult to do this with loved ones but you cannot afford to sacrifice your sanctity. Otherwise you'll settle on what you are given instead of you're supposed to have.

Actio is & Reflections

Can you think of anyone in your life who makes your feel uneasy or tense when around you? Or perhaps there's just an intuitive feeling you experience. That person needs to go.

It's perfectly okay to explain your actions to someone and to tell them why they can no longer experience your energy. Perhaps that person has no idea of the negative vibrations they're exuding. You may end up resolving the issue right there. Use your communication skills.

In some instances, you may be an influential person in which you can use that power to motivate people to positivity and to translate their energy into a frequency that is harmonious.

BE SENSITIVE TO PEOPLE.
STOP BEING SO SENSITIVE.

Be sensitive to people's feelings, dreams, conditions, energy…it's not about you.

Stop being so sensitive to what people say and/or think about your feelings, dreams, conditions, energy…it's not about you.

ACKNOWLEDGE & RELEASE

I learned a long time ago that the longer you hold a grudge against someone in your life, you won't truly be happy. Your energy is going towards projecting your expectations of "self" onto other people instead of accepting people for who they are. This will affect everything your life. Do not be fooled into thinking it's an isolated interaction.

Choose to be happy.

RELAX

When you're stressed, your energy affects everyone around you. Ask yourself, "What am I doing and who am I affecting with my energy?"

EVEN EXCHANGE

Surround yourself with people who not only are able to receive your energy but in turn, RETURN the energy back to you. So you have this constant flow of energy to and from your being. This is a special place to be and it takes a while to get your circle refined to this point but when you do, it's so blissful. This is part of the *harmony* I wrote about earlier. Often times we try to force interactions with people because we feel like we are obligated to create a bond after knowing someone for a short period of time. This should not be the case. Take your time and understand people. Ask questions about them. You'll find out if your puzzle pieces fit together or not.

DEALING WITH SOCIETAL NORMS

SUCCESS IS RELATIVE

Just like wealth and happiness. Remember this the next time you think about comparing your life to anyone else's. Their struggles are not yours. Own your cards and play them.

Actions & Reflections

How do you define 'success'?

_____

_____

Is your version of success determined by monetary worth?
Level of happiness? A combination?

_____

_____

CONVENTION DOES NOT CONSTITUTE SUCCESS

Just because something has been done a certain way for years, doesn't make it the best or most correct way of doing it. We are creatures of habit, so naturally we fall into complacency and routine. Societal norms are the compass for some, but it's okay to think freely. Try new ways of living. Be a pioneer.

AVOID CONFORMITY

No matter what they say or who doesn't "follow" you, don't conform. Remain convicted to everything you stand for while strengthening your mission. You WILL succeed.

LEARN TO APPRECIATE WHAT YOU HAVE WITHOUT FEELING GUILTY ABOUT IT

There will be times that you feel like you don't deserve what you have, or maybe you want to give everything you have to the less fortunate. It's okay to be grateful for what you've worked for (even given). Each person's situation is unique. The important idea to remember here is humility and selflessness. Giving back is necessary. Doesn't matter how much or how little. You don't need to publicize every time you help someone either. As long as you are trying to help someone else whenever you can (if you're in the position to), embrace the life you have

NO RULES TO LIFE

Marriage may not be for you, but you can still have love and a family. Religion may not be a part of your life, but you can still be a great person. College may not be in your plans, but you can still get an education and be successful. The point is this: don't subscribe to societal norms because of what you were conditioned to accept. Venture out and find what makes you happy, successful, and filled with light.

MARRIAGE

Marriage isn't for everyone.

A legal binding won't keep you together with someone. Not even children. Love, communication, and understanding (among many other things) are responsible for that. I'm a firm believer in this. I'm not interested in getting married and I've met plenty of men and women who feel the same. Having a child doesn't automatically constitute a marriage, nor does it make it ok for you to ask someone when their wedding date is. If you absolutely have to ask anything regarding that, maybe it should be, "How do you guys feel about marriage?"

I say that with reservation.

At least for Early Millennials (I'm 32), we were taught by media and our elders to grow up, get married, and start a family. In my opinion, women have had it worse with cartoon princesses/weddings, Jared's jewelry commercials, and let's not forget that this is the norm on tv shows and movies. The happy ending? The protagonist and his love interest get married. Or if the family is no longer together, the parents were once married. Someone is still wearing a ring, blah, blah, blah.

Rarely do you see families that are just…together. Simply together. With a strong bond and no marriage or ring in sight. I'm obviously bias and I know marriage is for some people and not for others. However, there's a gross imbalance of marriage in the media. As if to allude that is the best way to live.

I plan on having a family one day and marriage is not in that vision; something that I communicate up front when dating women. I find out her thoughts on marriage during conversation, and most of the time, my reasoning is understood. Occasionally, I'll get the, "Why not?" response. Thus, I reiterate myself, further breaking down the weakness of the institution while uplifting the bond that people can have.

To be clear, my best friend is married. I was his best man at his wedding and it was one of the most beautiful spectacles I've ever seen. I fully support him without question and I believe that their bond is strong. So it's not that I don't support marriage between two loving people, it's just that I don't support it being a stipulation to have a family or life for that matter.

Many of the reasons why I disagree with it come from overhearing women talk about engagement rings and how he better get a [insert carat size] rock. Huh? The ring size doesn't mean he loves you any more or less. That's vanity bullshit. You just want the attention. This isn't the case for every woman but I imagine that because you've succumbed to the societal pressures of the marital institution, your friends (not you) are expecting to see something worth discussing. So you need to get that huge rock on your fourth finger for people to see and talk about. I'm open to discussion about other reasons, but I fail to see what the ring size/type says about your partner's love for you. Let me reiterate that not all women are like this and at the same time, many men like partaking in this. Totally fine. I'm just pointing out some of the flaws with the process.

Another issue is the reason people get married and how soon they do it before really knowing the other person. I've seen a few situations where, because of the pressure from families and society, a couple gets married—without really knowing each other. When I lived in Atlanta for a while, I would hear stories or encounter people who were engaged but not living together or sharing the same space.

Most of the time this is a terrible idea unless you're over each other's houses ever other day. But the fact is, you need to know how that person: sleeps, eats, shits, pees, cooks, cares, and cleans in their home. And they need to know that about you. Paramount to that, you need to be able to do it together!

Getting married without really spending time with each other and being in each other's space is not the smartest move. There are always exceptions and I'm sure your brain is running through every married couple you know just so you can shout at me. I know. Relax. Generally speaking, you wouldn't buy car without test driving it. Why would you even think about marriage with someone whom you don't know very well.

On average, it costs approximately $25k for a typical American wedding. $25,000. Take into account the average cost of divorce being about $15k. You have the pressure put on as soon as you're out the gate. That's $40,000 worth as soon as you get going. So I can only imagine that many people force themselves to stay together because of the cost, if nothing else. Otherwise they live as "separated".

I don't want that pressure. I don't want to feel forced to stay with someone if I've fallen out of love with or perhaps are energies no longer work together and we're not compatible after all. Hopefully I make the right decision when the time comes but it will be love to keep me there, not legal documents, cost of divorce, and societal norms.

Whichever path you choose, go down that road for love, not because you feel pressured to do so.

THE HAPPINESS FACTOR

THE HAPPINESS FACTOR

Stated simply:

"A way of life that allows one to remain true to the journey. One achieves this by allowing happiness to be their motivation rather than what society deems 'successful'. Those who subscribe to this lifestyle remain conscious."

Let's break this down.

What I'm not saying: that your journey is not authentic and that your experience is not valid.

What I am saying: that we experience so much noise, pressure, and persuasion from the societal radio that we lose ourselves in the midst of trying to please everyone BUT are ourselves.

Happiness comes from you being healthy; in mind, body,

and spirit. If we lack in these areas, how can we expect to give to the people around us. Your job requires top notch work ethic. Your relationships require time and nurturing. —understanding. How can we give of ourselves if we have nothing to give?

Everything of course starts within right? So we must take a look at our situation.

Are you happy with your current job? If not, what would you require to allow you to enjoy it? Before you answer that, try to avoid saying "money". Money is a crutch and illusion that when presented in enough amounts, feels like it will solve all of your problems. That is false. The need for money is a symptom of a deeper issue. Perhaps a mismanagement of it is the real issue.

Whatever the case may be:
1. Scrutinize your situation
2. Decide what you need in order to make the situation better or to resolve an issue
3. If a solution cannot be derived or the situation too toxic, remove yourself from said situation.

If it matters, exhaust all options in step #2 before moving to the final step.

NEXT STEPS: CHALLENGES

In this last section, I'm going to a list a set of challenges for you to achieve. You can choose to do any or all of them…it's for you not me. However, as you complete them, make sure to either send me an email or tag the challenge number on social media along with #FindingOneChallenges.

1. Practice saying this to yourself everyday, even if you aren't fully convinced at first: "I am awesome!". Or if want to take it up a level, "I am fucking awesome!" I usually go with the latter.

2. Go out to that restaurant/bar/lounge (place) you've been wanting to go to…but go solo. Take yourself on a date and enjoy that time.

3. While doing action #2, talk to a stranger. Get at least one person's name. Whether it's the bartender (too easy since they want your money) or the person next to you (more challenging).

4. Go to a park or quiet place outdoors and just sit. Be.

5. Go to a coffee shop or walk around your city…without your phone! Leave that thing at home.

6. Give to/do something for someone without expectation of anything in return.

7. Call that person you've been thinking about. Or the next person that comes to mind.........now! Yea that person. Go. Why are you still reading this?

8. Learn something new every week and keep track of what it is your learning.

9. Teach someone something you know about or have learned recently. This allows us to strengthen our knowledge of a topic when we teach it to others.

10. Write a list of all the things that fill you with elation. Things that you crave to experience and enjoy. Either because you have or because you want to. Look at that list every day when you wake up. You'll see what happens.

11. Tell the people that have been there for you that you are grateful for their presence and support.

12. Send an email/tweet/comment to three hard to reach people you want to connect with offline. Cultivate that interaction. Try and do whatever you need to (legally) to get in touch. You can think Timothy Ferris* for this one.

13. Give a high five to a stranger (the high five is back in action people)

14. Commit a random act of kindness to someone you don't know or who is in need. And do it without sharing or recording it for social media posting. Don't talk about it at all. Make this a habit.

15. Travel outside of your city/state/country and explore some place you've never been or always wanted to go. We learn so much by traveling, even if it's only an hour or two away from you.

16. Go camping. Spend the night in the forest and wilderness at least once in your life. Our connection with nature is so important for balance and humanity. Touch the trees, smell flowers, and listen to the sounds of everything around you.

17. Eat some donuts (be it vegan or not)…do it for me!

18. Organize a get together or some kind of event. There's no better feeling than being able to bring people together through something that you have planned out. Could be a birthday party, a game night, or just a dinner with you and a couple friends. Who knows, it may turn into a "thing" that you continue to do regularly.

19. Share/buy this book for a friend you think would benefit from it (shameless I know but with the best intentions).

* Timothy Ferris is best known for his book, *The Four-Hour Work Week*. Information listed in the next section.

BOOKS TO READ

The Four-Hour Work Week: Escape 9-5, Live Anywhere, and Join the New Rich by Timothy Ferriss

Rich Dad, Poor Dad: What The Rich Teach Their Kids About Money - That The Poor And Middle Class Do Not! by Robert T. Kiyosaki

Influence: The Psychology of Persuasion by Robert B. Cialdini, PH.D.

The Definitive Book of Body Language by Barbara Pease & Allan Pease (one of my favorites)

Perfect Phrases for Dealing With Difficult People by Susan F. Benjamin

The Four Agreements: A Practical Guide to Personal Freedom by Don Miguel Ruiz

The Gentle Art of Verbal Self-Defense by Suzette Haden Elgin

CONNECT WITH ME

- Email: info@mrdabney.com
- Blog: http://mrdabney.com
- My software company, Empty Box Media:
  http://emptyboxmedia.com
- Instagram: @mrdabney
- Twitter: @vaughndabney
- Facebook Page: http://fb.me/TheVaughnDabney

Following me on any of these platforms does not mean I will reciprocate (see #6 in the Challenges section) however, I do appreciate all support!

Vaughn Dabney

ISBN: 1489536396
ISBN-13: 978-1489536396

Made in the USA
Lexington, KY
17 January 2017